AF287102

Pearl Substance

- Who Am I? -

Also from Nina Kristiina Honkanen

Towards the Golden Light Bird
– Consciousness Song for Treasure Seekers –

Pearl Substance

- Who Am I? -

Nina Kristiina Honkanen

Book cover: Arja Turunen, Graphic Studio Fenix
Layout: Nina Kristiina Honkanen

www.ninakristiinahonkanen.com

Publisher: BoD – Books on Demand, Helsinki, Finland
Manufacturer: BoD – Books on Demand, Noderstedt, Germany

ISBN: 978-952-802-148-3

For Markéta

Contents:

~ Prologue ~

"The Hymn of the Pearl", also known as "The Hymn of the Soul", is a poem belonging to Syrian and Greek manuscripts of *The Acts of Thomas* that is part of the gnostic apocryphal scripts left out of the main canon of the Bible, the authoritative collection of Jewish and early Christian texts. In *The Acts of Thomas* the apostle Thomas sings the Hymn as he prays for himself and his fellow prisoners.

In this booklet I have adapted "The Hymn of the Pearl" to better show my own interpretive understanding of the text while honouring the message of the original as closely as possible. "The Hymn of the Pearl" has been an important source of personal inspiration for many years. From the depth of my heart I hope this little booklet will awaken a deeper interest in the Hymn and maybe even become an inspiration to others with its message!

"The Hymn of the Pearl" is simple, yet profound and answers four important questions that have preoccupied the minds of each of us at times:

Who am I? Where do I come from? Why am I here? Where am I going?

To be mindful of these questions has the potential to open the locks of our hearts and minds through which we get glimpses of our true essence behind all lower thoughts and emotions. This brings peace, joy, and purpose to our experience of life.

Through this booklet my message to you, dear reader is, no matter what our situation or where we find ourselves, we should never give up hope. We are here on planet Earth as if in a schoolhouse learning to transform the "substance of our life" into what I will call *pearl substance*, the building material for our true essence, *the Light body* that will, ultimately, enable us to make the journey back to where we came from. In all our life experiences there is potential for this building material if we just wake up from the "sleep" of unconsciousness and ignorance and start seriously seeking our treasure, the reconnection to the Higher Light and Love!

Why is this reconnection important? – Without it, we cannot solve the problems of humanity!

Nina Kristiina Honkanen

Helsinki, Nov. 22, 2019

"If you know your origin,

you know your destiny."

J.J. Hurtak

- Who am I? -

Am I the little boy

who my mother calls

the little man, the golden jay

but who in the mind of the auntie next door

transforms to a "monster"

because she is disturbed

by the sounds of life each and every day.

Am I the small golden crumb

as my father calls me,

the sunshine, the little princess

whose funny stories, creativity,

and sweetness

make the boys in her class

tease her during recess?

Or am I the hungry child in poor homes,

the mistreated child,

the suffering child in many wars

who doesn´t have any good chances

to even know what to long for

and who just by biting her teeth together

manages in excruciating circumstances?

Am I, in other words,

the Matthew or the Mary,

the little child

of either good or bad conditions

who just by chance is here and now

and like this,

either "special" or "ordinary"?

Can I blame happenstance for my birth?

Is it the Darwinistic evolution

that generates the human being on Earth?

Am I just flesh belonging

to a fleshy bloodline?

Is my birth here the only time?

Is it only the growth of my brain,

my intelligence

that is the most important factor,

or is it about the fire of my emotions

that I can say the same?

Am I just what this society

wants me to believe;

what I can read from the school books

or what the mainstream media,

politicians, priests, academics, scientists,

or parents tell me?

Did I come from the earth,

and is my final stop the same?

Is it from the "dust"

that I started growing?

Is it the "dust"

that is the name of the game?

Am I a sinner saved only

through certain conditions?

Are there only Heaven, Hell, and Earth?

Am I not allowed to have

higher aspirations?

Was I born here only to work my butt off

and to suffer exceedingly

or to seek pleasure,

to compete against everyone

and everything,

and to gather earthly treasure?

Or is the meaning of my life

just to wait for the end

after which there is nothing?

Am I here to deprive others work

and the nature of this planet;

to be concerned only about my own gain,

or to try to be a good person;

to stay pure and blamelessly sane,

or to invent a way to stop the time;

so I could be forever

young, carefree, and without pain?

Is my purpose time after time

to clone myself; to become immortal

through technology,

through gene manipulation

or to build a magnificent

"hybrid superhuman being"

who doesn´t know pain nor capitulation

and whose weaknesses

are never shown in any situation?

Or is my purpose amazing rockets to build

that can fly to the stars faster than light

and in case of global catastrophe,

to transfer humanity to other planets,

to arrange a large scale flight?

* * *

- Hymn of the Pearl -

Or am I the King´s son

who grew up in the Great East

and who already in young age

was given a large responsibility:

who was sent far away to Egypt

to fetch the Pearl of Great Cost

and to lull the Serpent,

the guardian of the pearl,

to slumber so he wouldn´t even notice

what he´d lost?

Whose Parents made a covenant with him

and so that he wouldn´t forget it,

wrote in his heart:

if you succeed, with your Brother,

our next in rank,

shalt thou be heir in our Kingdom.

Did I part

from the Great Kingdom of the East?

Did I leave my glorious robe behind?

Did I take off my purple toga

that was woven to match with my stature

and was beautiful, to say the least?

Were there two guardians guiding me

on my scary way to Egypt?

Did they help me

on my long and dangerous journey

to fetching the Pearl of Great Cost

and to lulling the Serpent,

the guardian of the pearl,

to slumber so he wouldn´t even notice

what he´d lost?

Did they leave me alone in Egypt

where I met my kinsman,

an anointed one from the East

who became my companion

and warned me

not to be related with the strangers,

or my mission would be ceased?

Did I put on their alien clothing

because I was Heaven sent

and didn´t want them

to notice I was different?

Was it the Egyptians who tricked me

to eat their heavy food

and who ensnared me to serve their king,

to fall asleep, and to forget

who I was, where I had come from,

why I was here, and where I was going?

Was it my Father, the King of Kings,

my Mother, the Queen of the East,

and my Brother, the Crown Prince,

in the Kingdom of the East

who noticed the predicament I was in,

who wrote me a Letter

and prayed for me, ever since?

Was it them who urged me to wake up,

to rise up from my sleep,

to remember my glorious garment

and my marvellous toga,

and to start again my quest

to fetching the Pearl of Great Cost

and to lulling the Serpent,

the guardian of the pearl,

to slumber so he wouldn´t even notice

what he´d lost?

Was it my Father who sealed the Letter

with His right hand,

so that the wretched Babylonians

or the gruel demons of Sarbog

wouldn´t know its contents,

wouldn´t understand?

Was it in the form of an Eagle

that the Letter flew,

alighted beside me

and became all speech?

Was it the same words

that in the beginning

had been written into my heart

that now became alive for me

and answered my spiritual needs?

Did I kiss the Letter? Did I read it

and make it understandable for me?

Was it the echo of its Voice

that raised me up from my sleep?

- yes -

I remembered at last

why I had come to Egypt:

to fetch the precious Pearl of Great Cost

and to lull the Serpent,

the guardian of the pearl,

to slumber so he wouldn´t even notice

what he´d lost.

I uttered over him,

the Name of my Father,

the Name of my Mother,

and the Name of my Brother,

the Crown Prince;

it made him, the Serpent, disabled

and drowsy ever since.

I snatched away my precious Pearl,

the unclean clothes I left behind,

and as I turned back to the Great East,

my glorious garments I already saw

in my mind.

I beheld before me

the glowing fire letters,

the reddish shimmer of the Love Letter

that had awakened me from my sleep

that now, over and over,

encouraged me with its Voice,

guided me with its Light,

draw me onward with its Love

towards my Father´s House

that now, had become my priority.

The demons of Sarbog

and the wretched ones of Babylon

I left behind

as I reached to the great Mesene

at the seashore

where my Parents had sent

my toga and my garment.

I had been a child when I left

my Father´s House,

so I didn´t remember the value
of them anymore.

The hands of the King returned
through the hands of the treasurers
my deposit
– my true treasure –
when they brought back my garment
that was appropriately made
according to its value
in exactly the right measure.
The whole Image of the King of Kings
was embroidered
and in full all over it depicted.
I also saw it was adorned
with glorious stones and colours
as I stretched forth and received it.

The garment was like a mirror image of me:

in it I saw all of me and in me all of it.

We had been two in distinction,

and yet again, we were one in one likeness

now as we met

after Aeons of separateness.

My glorious garment pulsated

motions of knowledge

when it descended to me,

and I heard him sing:

"Look, this is him the active in deeds

whose works waxed my stature

by the Throne of my King!"

In its kingly movements,

it poured itself entirely over me,

and even I stretched out my hand
and ran to meet my glorious garment
as well as my bright-coloured toga;
my entire adornment.

Clothed in my garments, I went up
to the gate of peace and salutation
and did homage and bowed my head
to my Father´s Glory.
I had kept His commandments,
and even He kept His word
– remembered what He´d said:
He received me, rejoiced,
and gave me a place in His Kingdom,
in the court of His royals,
among His princes and nobles
where His servants sang

songs of praise to Him:

"Holy, Holy, Holy!"

He, my Brother, the Crown Prince,

promised I can now come

to the Court of the King of Kings

and with my offering and my Pearl

show up to our King with Him.

* * *

- Pearl Substance -

Hear, Oh Beloved Child of God:

When you into the *Image* and *Similitude*

of *Yod-Hey-Wod-Hey* were created,

you were granted

your wondrous *Garment of Light*

that through the Aeons has been

forgotten and underrated

even though it is your birthright.

A precious mission you were given:

to come to this world

to fetch the *Pearl of Great Cost*

and to lull the tenacious

pearl guarding Serpent to sleep,

so he wouldn´t even notice

what he´d lost.

The great price of the Pearl

comes from the fact

that you had to leave your shining garment

and your purple toga behind,

which was the pact

with you Parents in the East,

and before you would meet again,

be separated for Aeons,

many lives, at least.

- - -

So, we all fell asleep of oblivion

when we took the energy

of the Serpent inside,

– the lower thought substance –

that filled our whole being

with false knowledge and half-truths

interfering with the mission of our soul

by giving everything a lower meaning.

But the Love-Letter from our Father
– The Power of the Sacred Word –
can awaken us,
and if we truly assimilate its message,
many Sparks are gathered thus.

Then the energy of the Serpent inside
is like a parasite inside a mussel
that starts building a pearly substance
that transforms the disturber completely
into a precious pearl
- unbelievably neatly.

In other words,
all the "substance of our life" on Earth

can be the building material

– pearl substance –

for our precious *Light body*

in this endless Light continuum

of being and becoming

because who we truly are

is:

... I Am that I am ...

or

... I shall Be what I shall Be ...

... Ehyeh Asher Ehyeh ...

... Ain Soph! ...

* * *

- Acknowledgements -

Thank you, Markéta, for sharing this life with me and our son. Thank you for everything that you have done for this family! Thank you for your loving kindness, your sense of responsibility, your trustworthiness, and enormous strength and resilience. I love you deeply.

I also thank you, my family of Light on Earth, for your love and for sharing this gift of life and path of Light together with me!

But most of all I thank You, our Father and our Mother of the Infinite Light and our Brother, the Christ, for Your Love-Letter, the Sacred Word that is guiding us with the Love of its Living Light and the Living Light of its Love back to our Divine Family, our true home!

* * *

Glossary:

The numbers after the glossary words refer to the "Sources of Inspiration" list.

Ain Soph – (Hebrew) |4| The Name of God that signifies the Infinite, the Unlimited, the Unbounded, literally "No End". |7| Also the Source of All.

Egypt – Our material, dualistic world.

Ehyeh Asher Ehyeh – (Hebrew) |1| I Am that I Am or I Shall Be what I Shall Be.

Great East/Kingdom of the East – The Higher Heavens, the Kingdom of God.

I Am that I Am - |1| *Ehyeh Asher Ehyeh* (Hebrew) is the highest statement that a mortal can use in this world. It expresses the "covenant" between the human-self and the Christed Overself, and a knowing of one´s true identity, one´s destiny, and the keys to the higher thresholds.

Image and Similitude - |5| *Batsalmaynu – Kidmoothenu* (Hebrew). The Image is connected with our genetic blueprint that in turn is connected with *Adam Kadmon*, the Man/Woman of Light or the Heavenly blueprint of Man before the fall. The Similitude is the energy vibration that links us with the Divine.

Light - |2, 3| Light with a capital "L" is Higher Light, Super-Light that manifests continual creativity carrying the Codes and Thought-Forms of Light.

Light body - |2, 3| Body of higher energy experience that can participate in the Infinite Way of many realms or universes.

Pearl of Great Cost (or Price) - |6| Symbol for rediscovering the Light body; for processing and transforming the "substance of our life" into *pearl substance,* the building material for the Light body.

Serpent (or Snake) – Symbolic of the vehicle of the fallen mind energies, the lower forces that have been blocking our way to enliven the Truth.

Yod-Hey-Wod-Hey - יהוה (Hebrew letters are read from right to left), see *Keys of Enoch®*, Key 202. |1| YHWH is the revealed Name to our Father Universe of the Living God behind all Creator Gods. |4| The Divine Name of God that exemplifies the original coding mechanism for our physical body. The three letters in four places are the original blueprint, the "God Code" for the four bases of the DNA in our bodies, the code behind our Adamic species.

Sources of Inspiration:

1. The Book of Knowledge: The Keys of Enoch®, J.J. Hurtak, 1973
2. The First Light Picture Superscript: The Keys of Enoch® and Metatron, J.J. Hurtak, 1973, 2016
3. The Second Light Picture Superscript: The Keys of Enoch® and Metatron, J.J. Hurtak, 1973, 2017
    (There are two more Light Picture Super-scripts published and six subsequent ones waiting to be published)
4. The Overself Awakening, J.J. and Desiree Hurtak, 2011
5. The Seventy-Two Living Divine Names of The Most High, J.J. Hurtak, 2009
6. Seven Seals of Initiation and The Acts of Thomas - CD, J.J. Hurtak, 2004, the original audio cassette, 1975
7. The Holy Sephiroth and The Keys of Enoch, a teaching on seven levels, J.J. Hurtak, 1999
8. Pistis Sophia, A Coptic Gnostic Text with Commentary, J.J. and Desiree Hurtak, 1999
9. The Future of Humanity: Terraforming Mars, Interstellar Travel, Immortality and

Our Destiny Beyond Earth, Michio Kaku, 2018

10. Towards the Time of the Golden Light Bird – Consciousness Song for Treasure Seekers, Nina Kristiina Honkanen, 2020

11. "Tuomaan tekojen Helmihymni", *Nag Hammadin kätketty viisaus*, gnostilaisia ja muita varhaiskristillisiä tekstejä ("The Hymn of the Pearl of The Acts of Thomas", *The Hidden Wisdom of Nag Hammadi*, Gnostic and other early Christian texts in Finnish), WSOY, 2006

12. "Hymn of the Pearl", the translation of the Syrian text to English by William Wright, 1871 and the translation of the Greek text to English by G.R.S. Mead, 1900